TRAUMA

ISBN 978-3-9502910-5-6

„Life doesn't play by the rules.“

SCHEMA 2.3

„Play by your own rules.“

SCHEMA 2.3

Schema 2.2 was published with:
2.1 J.R. Carpenter · Generation[s] · Code Narrative
2.2 Ivan Monroy Lopez · git2pod · Poetry

Audun Mortensen

Surf's Up (2010)

first edition 2010
second edition 2013
third edition 2014

This book is only available at the online shop of Trauma Wien.
http://traumawien.at – verlag@traumawien.at

This book was set in Perpetua.
cover: Luc Gross & Julian Palacz
production: Julian Palacz
edit: Luc Gross

.com for Murder (2002)

In cyberspace no one can hear you scream.

3 Ninjas: High Noon at Mega Mountain (1998)

Saving the day the ninja way.

Abortion, The (2006)

Congratulations, it's a girl!

Addiction (2004)

Alien from L.A. (1988)

Venture to the core!

Tinseltown Was No Comparison
To The Underground.

The people at the center of the
earth are about to get a visitor.

Kathy Ireland is the Alien From L.A.

A fantastic adventure.

Alone in the Dark (2005)

Evil awakens.

Can mankind defeat the army of darkness unleashed by an ancient evil cult?

American Ninja V (1993)

The Magic Power of the Ninja Is About to Reveal Itself...

Anne B. Real (2003)

ANNE FRANK meets 8 MILE.

Another Nine & a Half Weeks (1997)

On the trail of an old love, he found
a dangerous new obsession.

Anus Magillicutty (2003)

The Anti-Movie that Anti-Matters!

Tastes Great, Less Feeling!

Apocalypse, The (2007)

Baby Geniuses (1999)

Think innocent. Think helpless.
Think again. Naps are history.

Barbaric Beast of Boggy Creek, Part II, The (1985)

The Legend Too Monstrous
To Die… Surfaces Again.

Battlefield Earth: A Saga of the Year 3000 (2000)

Prepare For Battle.

Take Back The Planet.

Prepare to go Psychlo.

On May 12, We Fight Back.

Beast of Yucca Flats, The (1961)

Commies made him an atomic mutant!

Ben & Arthur (2002)

Love calms the soul… and so does revenge.

Blade Master, The (1984)

A pure action fantasy where good, strength and exotic beauty battle evil.

A pure action fantasy.

Warrior, Magician, Hero, Thief. They called him… The Blade Master.

Body in the Web (1960)

A handful of girls enslaved by a diabolical human beast on an island where there is no way out…

The MONSTER is terror-crazed
by his deathly fear of fire!

Blood-Curdling! Hair-Raising! Spine-Chilling!

One bite from a giant spider turned him
into THE WORLD'S MOST HIDEOUS
MONSTER with a diabolical lust to KILL!

He strangles his victims with
his mammoth claws!

SO TERRIFYING AND SHOCKING you
will be frightened out of your wits!

Shock upon shock! Terror upon terror!

Craving the Blood of Beautiful Women!

Car 54, Where Are You? (1994)

Chairman of the Board (1998)

Work sucks!

Cool as Ice (1991)

When a girl has a heart of stone, there's only one way to melt it. Just add Ice.

Creeping Terror, The (1964)

Crossover (2006)

Play by your own rules.

Daddy Day Camp (2007)

The summer is going to be in tents.

Daniel the Wizard (2004)

Demon Island (2002)

A Weekend To Dismember.

You don't get voted off this island,
you get slaughtered off.

Die Hard Dracula (1998)

To kill the unkillable, one step at a time.

Dis - en historie om kjærlighet (1995)

Disaster Movie (2008)

Not another shallow Hollywood movie.

Better get off quick.

Al Gore was right.

Mother-@!#$@#^% Nature.

You’re favorite movies are going to be destroyed.

Rock on!

Destroying the summer… one movie at a time.

Prepare to die… laughing.

Ed (1996)

Minor league. Major friendship.

Heroes come in all shapes and sizes.

Eegah (1962)

The Crazed Love of a Prehistoric Giant
for a Ravishing Teenage Girl!

Eegah had never seen a girl until one fell
into his arms! Boy fights giant for girl prize!
Desert dune buggy first time on screen!

Primitive Passions Turned On! Love
Breaks the Time Barrier!

The name written in blood!

Emret komutanim: Sah mat (2007)

Epic Movie (2007)

We Know It's Big. We Measured.

The mother of all spoofs.

From 2 of the 6 writers of "Scary Movie".

Fat Slags (2004)

Feel the Noise (2007)

Dream out loud.

You've stepped up and stomped the yard, now get ready to get down and feel the power of the hottest hip-hop movie hit.

Final Sacrifice, The (1990)

On this mission, no sacrifice is too great!

A lost city… A cult of unholy warriors… And a boy's quest for the secret of his father's death.

From Justin to Kelly (2003)

The tale of two American Idols.

Furry Vengeance (2010)

He came. He saw. They conquered.

Gigli (2003)

The movie everyone is talking about. The couple everyone wants to be (Australian DVD cover).

Murder. Blackmail. Temptation.
Redemption. It's been a busy week.

Life doesn't play by the rules.

Cool as Ice (1991)

The glitz and glamor of being a big time Hollywood Go-Go dancer looked good from a distance, but up-close it was another story… this story.

She Murdered for Fame, but the Price Tag Was Too Much!

She Hungered For Fame…The Men In Her Life Offered Love, Danger, Excitement!

Vibrant… Unpredictable…

A girl tries to become the top star in the glamorous world of Go-Go Dancing.

Glitter (2001)

In music she found her dream, her love, herself.

A strength to survive. A desire to dream.

Going Overboard (1989)

In the world of comedy, it's sink or swim.

The love boat was never quite like this.

Hababam Sinifi 3,5 (2006)

Hillz, The (2004)

All is not quiet up in the suburbs.

Hobgoblins (1988)

Be careful what you wish for…
You just might get it!

Hottie & the Nottie, The (2008)

That's hot. That's not.

Love never needed to be so blind.

She's hot. She's not. He's nuts.

House of the Dead (2003)

The Dead Walk…You Run.

The game has just begun!

You won't last the night.

How do you kill something that's already dead? Any… way… you… can!

Are you dead or alive?

Humans versus zombies. Whose sides are you?

In the Mix (2005)

Everyone wants a piece of his action.

Welcome To The Family.

They've created a mobster!

Incredibly Strange Creatures Who Stopped Living and Became Mixed-Up Zombies!!?, The (1964)

She Keeps Monsters in Cages for Pets!
He Preys on Wild Go-Go Girls!

SEE: the dancing girls of the carnival murdered
by the incredible night creatures of the midway!
SEE: the hunchback of the midway fight a
duel of death with the mixed up zombies!
SEE: the world's first monster musical!

We Dare You to Remain Seated when
Monsters Invade Audience! Who'll
Chicken Out First--Boys or Girls? Girls!
Learn if Your Boy Friend Can Take It!

World's Weirdest Movie!

A Horrifying Movie of Weird Beauties
and Shocking Monsters...

1001 weirdest scenes ever!

Don't come if you're chicken!

At last a new kind of monster movie!

MONSTERS COME REAL! CRASH
OUT OF SCREEN! INVADE AUDIENCE!
ABDUCT GIRLS FROM THEIR
SEATS! Not 3-D. Don't Miss It!

Not For Sissies!

It's Pat (1994)

Kazaam (1996)

The world's most powerful genie
has just met his match.

He's A Rappin' Genie With An Attitude…
And He's Ready For Slam-Dunk Fun!

Keloglan vs. the Black Prince (2006)

Kis Vuk (2008)

Hipp, Hopp, Jön…

Laserblast (1978)

Billy was a kid who got pushed around…
Then he found the power.

The Original Sci-Fi Classic!

Lawnmower Man 2: Beyond Cyberspace (1996)

God made him simple. Science made him a god. Now, he wants revenge.

Leonard Part 6 (1987)

America's best-dressed superspy!

His daughter is engaged to a man old enough to be his father. His estranged wife behaves like she is younger than their daughter. And now his government has asked him to save the world. Again.

Our world is in safe hands.

Action! Adventure! Aggravation!

Is this the man to save our planet?

Maize: The Movie, The (2004)

Manos: The Hands of Fate (1966)

It's Shocking! It's Beyond Your Imagination!

A cult of weird, horrible people who
gather beautiful women only to deface
them with a burning hand!

No one seated the last 10 minutes!
We defy you to guess the ending…
and ask you not to divulge it!

Meet the Spartans (2008)

The Bigger the Hit, The Harder They Fall.

Get Ready For the Next Big Epic Comedy.

300 had it coming (UK theatrical poster).

Merlin's Shop of Mystical Wonders (1996)

In a world where magic only
exists, anything can happen.

Miss Castaway and the Island Girls (2004)

There's trouble in paradise.

Mitchell (1975)

Murder… Cops… and Corruption.

Brute force with a badge.

…a tough, single-minded cop hot in pursuit…

When Mitchell is on the case… action
and excitement are job one!

A cop with a gun, a drink, and no friends.

Monster a-Go Go (1965)

The picture that comes complete with a 10-foot-tall monster to give you the wim-wams!

How did a 10-foot-tall monster get into that little bitty space capsule?

You've Never Seen a Motion Picture Like This -- Thank Goodness!

A way-out tale of a far-out monster!

An astronaut went up -- a "guess what" came down!

Night Train to Mundo Fine (1966)

Make the Mistake!

Nine Lives (2002)

Their number is up!

Phat Girlz (2006)

Her dreams are about to get a whole lot bigger.

She's proving that BIG is beautiful.

Pledge This! (2006)

Pledging Has Never Been This Hilarious.

Pocket Ninjas (1997)

They're the funniest fiercest fighting
force under four feet.

Pod People, The (1983)

Men were not ready to meet these…

An extra-terrestrial from the forbidden zone.

Popstar (2005)

He's topped the charts. Can he top high school?

Prince of Space (1959)

When an alien force tries to invade Earth to steal a powerful new rocket fuel, a mysterious hero intervenes.

Pumaman, The (1980)

Ram Gopal Varma Ki Aag (2007)

Santa Claus (1959)

An Enchanting World of Make-Believe!

Bursting upon our BIG SCREEN in all the colors of the rainbow... a prize-winning blue ribbon treat for old and young alike! Here's something for the whole family to see together!

See All the Weird and Wonderful Characters of Make-Believe! The Fantastic Crystal Work-Room of the Happy Elves! The Fabulous Realm of the Candy-Stick Palaces!

At Last a Movie That's All About Him!

Better Than a Visit from Saint Nick Himself!

Santa Claus Conquers the Martians (1964)

Blast off for Mars… with Santa and a pair of Earth kids! Blast off for Mars… with Santa and a pair of Earth kids! Science-Fun-Fiction at its height!

Santa Claus saves Christmas for the Children of the World!

Santa Kidnapped by the Martians! Out-of-this-world fun 'n' action… as two Earth Kids are whisked away with him to Mars!

SEE: The Martians Kidnap Santa! Santa's North Pole Workshop! The Fantastic Martian Toy Factory! Earth Kids Meeting with Martian Kids! Space-ship Journey from Earth to Mars! Santa Turn Mars-Robot Into a Mechanical Toy!

Blast off for Mars… with Santa and a pair of Earth kids!

Santa Brings Christmas Fun to Mars!

Santa with Muscles (1996)

He's naughty, He's nice, and He's coming to save Christmas.

He's arrived in the St. Nick of time!

Simon Sez (1999)

The game's not over until…

It Ain't Over Til… (Simon Sez).

Skydivers, The (1963)

I like coffee!

Thrill jumping guys… thrill seeking gals… daring death with every leap!

First feature length motion picture showing the daredevils of the sky who free fall from heights of 20,000 feet with only a ripcord between life and death!

Smokers, The (2000)

They started something they couldn't end.

Looking for love, they called it a revolution…

Snowboard Academy (1996)

The path to higher education is all downhill!

Son of the Mask (2005)

Who's next?

The next generation of mischief.

The Power of Mischief.

Sequel to the #1 box-office hit.

Soultaker (1990)

There is no Stairway to Heaven.

Trapped in the Twilight Between Life and Death.

Space Mutiny (1988)

There is nowhere to hide from the enemy within!

Starfighters, The (1964)

The blazing adventure of the men and planes who rocket to the very edge of outer space!

Stjerner uden hjerner (1997)

Superbabies: Baby Geniuses 2 (2004)

The New Dirty Dozen…Time For A Change!

Meet the new generation of superheroes.

Don't drive, crawl!

America's favorite talking babies are back.

Surf School (2006)

This summer get wet!

American Pie at the beach… in Costa Rica. Surf's up!

Tangents (1994)

The Ultimate Time Transport must be
Destroyed to Save the Future...

His mission is to save the future.
But time waits for no man...

The times they are a changing...

Saving the future before time runs out...

Tony Blair Witch Project, The (2000)

The most important documentary… ever.

Track of the Moon Beast (1976)

The Rising Moon Creates A Monster.

Troll 2 (1990)

The original boogeyman is back.

Troppo Belli (2005)

Turks in Space (2006)

Who's Your Caddy? (2007)

This summer, it's the street vs. the elite.

Why Did I Get Married Too? (2010)

Marriage is an institution they're committed to.

Together. Forever.

Wild World of Batwoman, The (1966)

Beyond Wildest Dreams!

Super-heroine battles diabolical
evil to save the world!

Her thrills rip forth in wide wild adventure!

Zaat (1975)

Hydra will rip at your senses and plunge
you into a quagmire of revulsion…

Is the monster man… fish… or devil?

It would take an atom bomb to
wipe out the walking catfish!

A creature like you've never seen before.

Zeiten ändern Dich (2010)

Zodiac Killer (2005)

The 12 Signs of Evil.

Zombie Nation (2004)

Terror In Numbers.

www.ingramcontent.com/pod-product-compliance
Ingram Content Group UK Ltd.
Pitfield, Milton Keynes, MK11 3LW, UK
UKHW021642190726
13853UKWH00001B/3